Special Education Teacher

CAREERS WITH CHARACTER

Careers with Character

Special Education Teacher

by Ellyn Sanna

MASON CREST PUBLISHERS

Mason Crest Publishers Inc.
370 Reed Road
Broomall, Pennsylvania 19008
(866) MCP-BOOK (toll free)
www.masoncrest.com

1059084-327-4 (series)

First Edition, 2003
13 12 11 10 09 08 07 06 05 04   10 9 8 7 6 5 4 3 2

Library of Congress Cataloging-in-Publication Data on file at the Library of Congress.

Special Education Teacher
LC Control Number: 2002154722
Type of Material: Book (Print, Microform, Electronic, etc.)
Brief Description: Sanna, Ellyn, 1958-
Special education teacher / by Ellyn Sanna.
Broomall, Pa. : Mason Crest Publishers, c2003.
v, 90 p. : ill. (some col.) ; 25 cm.
ISBN: 1590843258
Call Number: LC3969 .S25 2003

Design by Lori Holland.
Composition by Bytheway Publishing Services, Binghamton, New York.
Produced by Harding House Publishing Service, Vestal, New York.
Printed and bound in the Hashemite Kingdom of Jordan.

CONTENTS

We each leave a fingerprint on the world.
Our careers are the work we do in life.
Our characters are shaped by the choices
we make to do good.
When we combine careers with character,
we touch the world with power.

INTRODUCTION

by Dr. Cheryl Gholar
and Dr. Ernestine G. Riggs

In today's world, the awesome task of choosing or staying in a career has become more involved than one would ever have imagined in past decades. Whether the job market is robust or the demand for workers is sluggish, the need for top-performing employees with good character remains a priority on most employers' lists of "must have" or "must keep." When critical decisions are being made regarding a company or organization's growth or future, job performance and work ethic are often the determining factors as to who will remain employed and who will not.

How does one achieve success in one's career and in life? Victor Frankl, the Austrian psychologist, summarized the concept of success in the preface to his book *Man's Search for Meaning* as: "The unintended side-effect of one's personal dedication to a course greater than oneself." Achieving value by responding to life and careers from higher levels of knowing and being is a specific goal of teaching and learning in "Careers with Character." What constitutes success for us as individuals can be found deep within our belief system. Seeking, preparing, and attaining an excellent career that aligns with our personality is an outstanding goal. However, an excellent career augmented by exemplary character is a visible expression of the human need to bring meaning, purpose, and value to our work.

Career education informs us of employment opportunities, occupational outlooks, earnings, and preparation needed to perform certain tasks. Character education provides insight into how a person of good character might choose to respond, initiate an action, or perform specific tasks in the presence of an ethical dilemma. "Careers with Character" combines the two and teaches students that careers are more than just jobs. Career development is incomplete without character development. What better way to explore careers and character than to make them a single package to be opened, examined, and reflected upon as a means of understanding the greater whole of who we are and what work can mean when one chooses to become an employee of character?

Character can be defined simply as "who you are even when no one else is around." Your character is revealed by your choices and actions. These bear your personal signature, validating the story of who you are. They are the fingerprints you leave behind on the people you meet and know; they are the ideas you bring into reality. Your choices tell the world what you truly believe.

Character, when viewed as a standard of excellence, reminds us to ask ourselves when choosing a career: "Why this particular career, for what purpose, and to what end?" The authors of "Careers with Character" knowledgeably and passionately, through their various vignettes, enable one to experience an inner journey that is both intellectual and moral. Students will find themselves, when confronting decisions in real life, more prepared, having had experiential learning opportunities through this series. The books, however, do not separate or negate the individual good from the academic skills or intellect needed to perform the required tasks that lead to productive career development and personal fulfillment.

Each book is replete with exemplary role models, practical strategies, instructional tools, and applications. In each volume, individuals of character work toward ethical leadership, learning how to respond appropriately to issues of not only right versus wrong, but issues of right versus right, understanding the possible benefits and consequences of their decisions. A wealth of examples is provided.

What is it about a career that moves our hearts and minds toward fulfilling a dream? It is our character. The truest approach to finding out who we are and what illuminates our lives is to look within. At the very heart of career development is good character. At the heart of good character is an individual who knows and loves the good, and seeks to share the good with others. By exploring careers and character together, we create internal and external environments that support and enhance each other, challenging students to lead conscious lives of personal quality and true richness every day.

Is there a difference between doing the right thing, and doing things right? Career questions ask, "What do you know about a specific career?" Character questions ask, "Now that you know about a specific career, what will you choose to do with what you know?" "How will you perform certain tasks and services for others, even when no one else is around?" "Will all individuals be given your best regardless of their socioeconomic background, physical condition, ethnicity, or religious beliefs?" Character questions often challenge the authenticity of what we say we believe and value in the workplace and in our personal lives.

Character and career questions together challenge us to pay attention to our lives and not fall asleep on the job. Career knowledge, self-knowledge, and ethical wisdom help us answer deeper questions about the meaning of work; they give us permission to transform our lives. Personal integrity is the price of admission.

The insight of one "ordinary" individual can make a difference in the world—if that one individual believes that character is an amazing gift to uncap knowledge and talents to empower the human community. Our world needs everyday heroes in the workplace—and "Careers with Character" challenges students to become those heroes.

Special education teachers see each child as unique and valuable.

1

JOB REQUIREMENTS

You don't have to wait until college
to prepare yourself for life.

Helen was an impossible child. Her family loved her very much, but they could not begin to teach her the skills she needed in order to rise above her disabilities. Helpless, frustrated, they allowed Helen to do as she pleased. Meanwhile, unable to hear or see, Helen was locked inside herself. An intelligent and loving child, her intelligence and affectionate nature were deeply hidden beneath her disabilities; on the surface, she was as unpleasant and surly as a wild animal. She desperately needed someone to show her a bridge across her handicap; she needed a teacher to help her connect with the world outside herself. But what teacher would want to take on the enormous challenge she presented?

A special teacher had the courage and other character qualities needed to show Helen Keller the way out of her dark, silent world. Annie Sullivan taught Helen not only how to behave appropriately with other people and how to manage the basic self-care tasks most of us take for granted; Annie also taught Helen how to communicate. Because of Annie, Helen Keller became an independent and creative woman, an author, speaker, and social activist who would one day win the Nobel Peace Prize. But without Annie Sullivan, the world would never have known all that Helen Keller had to offer.

Today special education teachers continue to help students with various disabilities. Through these teachers' compassion and diligence, children learn better ways to cope with the world around them; they become more independent members of our society; and the world has the chance to benefit from the unique gifts each individual has to offer.

When Helen Keller was a child, no public school existed that could have met her unique needs. Today, however, federal law requires public schools to provide children with disabilities a free and appropriate public education in the *least restrictive environment* appropriate to their individual needs. This law, the Education for All Handicapped Children Act of 1975 (or P. L. 94-142, today referred to as IDEA, the Individuals with Disabilities Education Act) means that many career openings exist in the field of special education. Children with disabilities cannot be hidden away at home or in institutions and private schools. Like any other child, they have the right to be taught by trained teachers who can address their unique needs.

This special approach to education requires a particular kind of training. Although no "magic formulas" exist that allow special education teachers to meet the unique challenges presented by children with disabilities, their training does prepare them to be able to focus on children rather than classrooms. Special education honors the unique value of every individual. While "regular" teachers often think most about the needs of groups of children, special education teachers must always see the needs of each separate child for whom they are respon-

---

The various types of disabilities that qualify for special education programs include:

- Learning disabilities
- Speech or language impairments
- Mental retardation
- Emotional disturbance
- Hearing impairments
- Orthopedic impairments
- Visual impairments
- Autism
- Deaf-blindness
- Traumatic brain injury
- Multiple disabilities and other health impairments

sible. As a result, they require a thorough understanding of a variety of teaching techniques and technology.

Special education teachers study these skills at both the undergraduate and graduate levels. Many colleges and universities across the United States and Canada offer programs in special education. Most bachelor's degree programs last four years and include both general education coursework and courses that focus specifically on special education. Courses include educational psychology, legal issues of special education, child growth and development, and the knowledge and skills needed to develop and teach curricula for students with disabilities. More and more colleges and universities are now also requiring an additional fifth year to receive an undergraduate degree in special education. Whether the program lasts four years or five, however, the final year is usually spent student teaching, gaining practical experience in a classroom supervised by a *certified* teacher.

> *The mystery of language was revealed to me [by my teacher]. I knew then that "w-a-t-e-r" meant the wonderful cool something that was flowing over my hand. That living word awakened my soul, gave it light, joy, set it free!*
> —Helen Keller

Like any other teacher in the United States and Canada, special education teachers must be certified. State boards of education or licensure advisory committees usually grant licenses, and the requirements vary from state to state within the United States and from province to province in Canada. All states and provinces require at least a bachelor's degree and the completion of an approved teacher preparation program. Many states also require that special education teachers obtain a master's degree in special education, which involves at least one year of additional course work. Some states and provinces have agreements that allow special education teachers to simply transfer their license from one place to another, but many states mandate that special education teachers pass the particular licensing requirements for that state. This may mean taking a comprehensive exam, or it may mean additional coursework to meet a state's differing requirements. In the future,

Children with disabilities may have difficulty learning to write basic letters and numerals.

ployers may come to recognize certification standards offered by a national organization.

Because of the great need to fill special education positions, emergency licenses are available in many states. If no teacher can be found who is certified in special education to fill a particular position, the state may grant an alternative license so that college graduates who are changing careers can enter the field more quickly. The requirements for these alternative licenses vary from state to state; in some cases, individuals begin teaching with a provisional certification that allows them one or two years to take the special education courses they need. This may not be the ideal route to take, for either the teacher or the students, since it means the teacher must plunge into a new field and learn from experience as she goes along. Coursework is a real and practical part of training to be a special education teacher.

However, a field like special education has requirements other than those that are purely academic. Annie Sullivan, for instance, the skilled teacher who was able to teach Helen Keller, had only a high school education—but she had 20 years of life experiences that had helped her build the character she needed to be a master teacher.

In our current world, Annie would have needed the proper education and certification, no matter how strong her character might have been. But today we sometimes go to the opposite extreme: we focus so much on academic preparation for a particular career that we forget how vital character is to professional success.

According to character education expert Tom Lickona, good character depends on possessing certain core values. We've mentioned a few of these values already—qualities like respect and compassion, self-discipline and diligence, responsibility, and courage. Other aspects of good character include integrity and trustworthiness, justice and fairness, and citizenship. These values affirm our dignity as human beings. Living out these values in our personal and professional lives is not only good for us as individuals; it is also good for the world around us. When we demonstrate these qualities in our lives, then we treat others the way we would each like to be treated. And by doing so, we help others, just as Annie Sullivan did. We make the world a better place.

Some children with disabilities may have trouble with math concepts.

If a child with a disability is able to function in a normal classroom, then that is the "least restrictive environment" required by federal law; however, she will probably still need the support of a trained special education teacher. Another child may need a self-contained classroom; his "least restrictive environment" will require the attention of a full-time special education teacher. More and more, however, researchers are finding that children with disabilities learn best when they have the opportunity to take part in "mainstreaming," participating in regular classroom activities. This does not mean that special education teachers are no longer needed, however; instead, it means that today's special education teachers will work closely with regular classroom teachers, ensuring that each child's individual needs are met by the educational program.

Annie Sullivan's character was forged out of hardship. She learned compassion and respect as she cared first for her younger brothers and sisters after their mother died, then for the younger inmates of the poorhouse where she was forced to reside when she was ten, and next for her fellow students at the school for the blind, which she attended from the time she was 14 until she graduated at 20; these same experiences also taught her many other valuable character lessons, and helped her to grow into the diligent and self-disciplined young woman who taught Helen Keller.

Few of us would choose to take the same hard route Annie did—but

Helen Keller could not have become a world-famous author and speaker without the help of her teacher.

we can each find opportunities in our own lives that will allow our characters to grow. We do not have to wait until we are in college to begin developing the skills that will make us effective in the careers we will one day follow. No matter how old we are or what our circumstances, we all have plenty of chances to honor the qualities that will make us people of character.

In the chapters that follow we will look at each of the character qualities we have mentioned:

- integrity and trustworthiness
- respect and compassion
- justice and fairness
- responsibility
- courage
- self-discipline and diligence
- citizenship

These values are played out in a unique way within the context of special education. As special education teachers demonstrate these character qualities, they have powerful opportunities to make our world a better place for all of us to live.

What lies behind us and what lies before us are small matters compared to what lies within us.

—Ralph Waldo Emerson

Children challenged with emotional disturbances benefit from a variety of learning opportunities—including, sometimes, the chance to be responsible for a pet.

2

INTEGRITY AND TRUSTWORTHINESS

*Sometimes when you try to choose
a moral path, you may see more than one
"right" way to go.*

Terry Kane, a special education teacher in a small, rural school, prides herself on being an honest person. But this year she found herself in a situation where being honest did not come easily. In fact, she needed to think a long time before she could even decide on a course of action that would most demonstrate integrity and trustworthiness.

Terry teaches a class of ***emotionally disturbed*** elementary children, ages nine to 11. Although she has only five children in her classroom, these children keep her busy from the moment she arrives at school until dismissal. The children's severe emotional problems mean that they must be monitored closely at all times.

For instance, Leesa, the only girl in Terry's class, has been through a series of foster homes; she was sexually abused by both her original father and by a foster parent, and although she is only nine, her conversation and behavior are full of sexual connotations. But Mark and Jeffie, two brothers, ages 11 and nine, seem oblivious to her actions. Jeffie, the younger brother is physically able to speak, but he has chosen not to ever since he saw his mother murdered by his father. Mean-

Special education teachers work with emotionally disturbed children in small groups.

while, Mark does the talking for his younger brother—in fact, Mark never *stops* speaking. He talks constantly about everything and anything, driving everyone around him crazy. LaMar, another 11-year-old in the group, is nearly as silent as Jeffie, although he will often mutter under his breath. Terry suspects that LaMar is abused at home, although so far she can prove nothing. However, she knows he cannot bear to be touched. Even a hand on his shoulder turns him into a snarling bundle of thrashing arms and legs. Sometimes as he sits hunched over his desk, Terry can almost see the anger and frustration seething under his skin. The smallest thing sends him into a rage, particularly, for some reason, the antics of Terry's fifth student, Nathan. Nathan comes from a stable home with loving parents, but ever since he was a toddler, he has not been like other children. He hears things no one else hears and he sees things no one else can see; he lives in a world of his own, and Terry often feels at a loss as she tries to counter the terrors and pleasures of Nathan's invisible world.

Despite the challenges presented by these students, Terry enjoys working with her class. Although each child tries her patience in one way or another, each child also delights her with his or her unique and quirky gifts. But as much as Terry likes her job, she's also grateful for the small breaks she has during her workday.

One of these breaks comes on Tuesdays and Thursdays, when the class has gym with Mr. Baker, the school's regular physical education teacher. Terry has explained to Jon Baker her students' learning requirements, and Jon has struggled to be cooperative. Terry senses, though, that his patience with these children is limited, and so she often picks them up a little early at the end of their gym class.

As she walked into the gym one day to collect her students, she found LaMar embroiled in an argument with Mr. Baker. Mr. Baker had apparently asked LaMar to pick up the balls from around the gym floor, but LaMar was unwilling to cooperate. Before Terry could intervene, Mr. Baker took LaMar's shoulder in a firm grasp to pull him toward the balls. Immediately, LaMar erupted in anger. He swung one small fist and slugged Mr. Baker in the arm. Just as quickly, Mr. Baker backhanded LaMar across the face.

"Look," Jon Baker told Terry that day after school. "I know I shouldn't have hit the kid. It was just instinct. I didn't mean for it to

> People who value integrity and trustworthiness:
>
> - tell the truth.
> - don't withhold important information.
> - are sincere; they don't deceive or mislead.
> - don't betray a trust.
> - don't steal.
> - don't cheat.
> - stand up for beliefs about right and wrong.
> - keep their promises.
> - return what they have borrowed and pay their debts.
> - support and protect their families, friends, community, and country.
> - don't talk behind people's backs or spread rumors.
> - don't ask their friends to do something wrong.
>
> Adapted from material from the Character Counts Coalition, 4640 Admiralty Way, Suite 1001, Marina del Rey, California 90292.

Teachers of emotionally disturbed youngsters need to be sensitive to students' feelings of anxiety, depression, and isolation.

happen, and it won't happen again. But I'm only a first-year teacher. I could lose my job here if you report what happened."

Terry knew that Jon Baker was truly sorry he hit LaMar—but Terry's school district requires that a teacher make an official report any time physical punishment is used within the school. Hitting children is no longer an acceptable punishment in either American or Canadian schools, and a professional accused of violence against a student may face serious consequences.

What should Terry do? Leesa and Mark seemed to have barely noticed the incident, and Terry knew neither Jeffie nor Nathan were capable of reporting what happened. LaMar himself was reluctant to discuss the incident in the gym; Terry suspected he was too worried about getting in trouble for

An *ethical dilemma* is a situation that demands we make a choice about what is the right thing to do. If we want to be people who value the qualities of good character, then we must take the time to sort out these ethical dilemmas carefully.

Emotionally disturbed children often have normal intelligence—but their disability may interfere with their ability to learn reading and other basic academic skills.

hitting a teacher to be concerned with reporting Mr. Baker's own violation of the rules. She wondered if LaMar might be so accustomed to being hit by adults that it never even occurred to him that Mr. Baker had done something wrong.

As a special education teacher—and as a person—Terry had run smack into one of the most common ethical dilemmas in the world: truth versus loyalty. She had to make a choice: should she tell the truth and report the incident in the gym? Or should she be loyal to a fellow teacher and protect him from the consequences of his actions?

Rushworth M. Kidder, the author of *How Good People Make Tough Choices,* writes that people often use three principles for resolving difficult dilemmas like the one Terry faced. These principles are:

1. Do what others want you to do. (This is referred to as "care-based" thinking.)
2. Do what's best for the greatest number of people. (This is called "ends-based" thinking.)
3. Follow your highest sense of what is right. (This is "rule-based" thinking.)

Terry used these principles as she struggled to sort out the situation. If she followed the care-based approach and did what others wanted her to do, then she supposed she would simply keep quiet and go on. That was what Jon Baker wanted her to do, after all, and no one else was expressing an opinion, since the only other people who even knew of the event were her students.

But then Terry began to wonder: what if others *did* know? Suppose her principal knew what had happened, or her district's Director of Special Education? What would *they* want her to do? But that was the whole point, wasn't it? They *didn't* know, and they wouldn't know, unless Terry told them—and if she told them, she would likely cost Jon Baker his job. Terry's head hurt as she tried to figure out what she should do.

Everyone makes mistakes, she reasoned, especially during their first year of teaching. She certainly had when she was a first-year

The four enemies of integrity:

- self-interest (The things we want . . . the things we might be tempted to lie, steal, or cheat to get.)
- self-protection (The things we don't want . . . the things we'd lie, steal, or cheat to avoid.)
- self-deception (When we refuse to see the situation clearly.)
- self-righteousness (When we think we're always right . . . an end-justifies-the-means attitude.)

Adapted from materials from the Josephson Institute of Ethics, 4640 Admiralty Way, Suite 1001, Marina del Rey, California 90292.

teacher; she would have hated to have each and every example of her poor judgment reported to her supervisor. Using ends-based thinking, she decided that the best thing for everyone would be to simply let the incident go.

And yet when she tried to put the whole thing out her mind, something still niggled at her conscience. Somehow she didn't feel honest not reporting what had happened. Maybe she needed to use "rule-based" thinking and listen to her own personal sense of what was right.

So she went through the entire dilemma one more time. This time she asked herself a different set of questions:

- Was it good for LaMar to think that adults were allowed to hit him?
- Was it good for the other children, whether they totally understood what had happened or not, to think that hitting had no consequences, so long as you were bigger or had more power?
- Was it good for Jon Baker to get away with no consequences for his behavior?

Three Foundations for Ethical Decision Making

1. Take into account the interests and well-being of everyone concerned. (Don't do something that will help you if it will hurt another.)
2. When a character value like integrity and trustworthiness is at stake, always make the decision that will support that value. (For example, tell the truth even though it may cost you some embarrassment.)
3. Where two character values conflict (for instance, when telling the truth might hurt another person), choose the course of action that will lead to the greatest good for everyone concerned. Be sure to seek all possible alternatives, however; don't opt for dishonesty simply as the easiest and least painful way out of a difficult situation.

Adapted from materials from the Josephson Institute of Ethics, 4640 Admiralty Way, Suite 1001, Marina del Rey, California 90292.

- What course of action did loyalty to her students demand of her?
- Who was most in need of her protection—Jon Baker or her students?
- Would she be betraying someone's trust if she told—or if she didn't?

What do you think Terry decided to do? What would you have done in her place?

Dare to speak the truth. If one life shines, the life next to it will catch the light.

—Anonymous

A special education teacher often uses computers to help supplement her students' learning.

3

RESPECT AND COMPASSION

*Not all ethical dilemmas are dramatic
crises. Some of them are ordinary moments
that can slip by without your ever
noticing . . . unless you're careful.*

G ary Rock thinks of himself as a kind guy. He's courteous with his
fellow teachers as he helps them meet the needs of the students
with special needs who are ***mainstreamed*** in their classrooms; he never
loses his temper with the group of middle school students for whom
he's responsible as a ***consultant teacher***. He fits himself respectfully
into many different kinds of classrooms, always striving to help the regular education teacher provide a better education for "his" kids. When
he meets with those students in small groups or one- on-one, he is usually patient and tolerant.

But this fall, as he prepared for a conference with the parents of one
of his students, he found himself struggling over what he would say.
Everything he could think of was negative.

Gary's 19 other parent-teacher conferences had been no problem.
He'd reassured Mrs. Carter that her son was making great gains as he
learned new techniques for dealing with his learning disability; he'd
gently helped Mr. and Mrs. Mead come to terms with the reality of their
daughter's handicap; and he'd helped Mr. Mintz see the positive side of
his son's character, despite the boy's many behavior problems. But

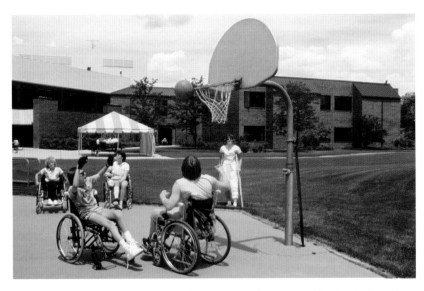

Even students with multiple handicaps can take part in physical education.

when it came to Randy Zondervan, Gary just couldn't think of anything good to say.

Randy, a student with multiple handicaps, was so large that he spilled out the sides of his wheelchair. Although he was capable of basic self-care, he usually smelled bad, because he hated to shower. He had a high squeaky voice that got on Gary's nerves, and he asked Gary the same questions over and over and over: *Do you have a dog, Mr. Rock? What's your dog's name, Mr. Rock? What does your dog look like, Mr. Rock? Is your dog fluffy? Is your dog brown? Is your dog a boy or a girl, Mr. Rock? What does your dog look like, Mr. Rock?*

For some reason, Randy was fascinated with dogs—and no matter how many times Gary told him about his dog, the next day (or the next period) Randy would want to know it all over again, and once again they would go through the whole cycle: *Do you have a dog, Mr. Rock? What's your dog's name, Mr. Rock? What. . . ?*

Randy was mildly retarded, and so Gary understood that schoolwork was a struggle for him—but Gary also knew that Randy was just too lazy to try. He'd rather sit in his wheelchair and ask any people within earshot about their dogs.

To Gary, Randy's laziness seemed to be the biggest problem he had, a worse problem than his physical handicap or his retardation, worse even than his obsession with dogs. Randy just couldn't be bothered to do much of anything. Gary had attempted to motivate him by working out a **behavior management** program, but Randy refused to cooperate. Gary had decided that when he met with Randy's parents, he would simply have to tell them the truth: their son was lazy.

But as he prepared for the meeting the following morning, his conscience nagged him. A parent-teacher conference wasn't really such a big deal, he told himself; it wasn't important enough for him to sit down and sort out what was right and wrong. After all, you couldn't look at it as though it were some sort of ethical dilemma.

Or could you? Gary decided to follow five steps for solving a moral choice.

1. Clarify

First, Gary had to admit he was faced with a moral choice. This was practically the hardest step of all for Gary to take. It would have been far easier for him to simply brush off the message his conscience was sending him. Instead of using his free period to prepare for the parent-teacher conference, he could have

People who value respect and compassion:

- are courteous and polite.
- are tolerant; they accept individuals' differences.
- don't mistreat or make fun of anyone.
- don't use or take advantage of others.
- respect others' rights to make their own decisions.
- are sensitive to others' feelings.
- live by the Golden Rule. (They treat others the way they want to be treated.)
- help others.
- share what they have with others.
- do what they can to help those who are in trouble.
- forgive others.

Adapted from material from the Character Counts Coalition, 4640 Admiralty Way, Suite 1001, Marina del Rey, California 90292.

Lack of sleep can add to a student's learning difficulties. Special education teachers need to be aware of their students' home situations; they may need to educate parents about what their children require in order to do better in school.

been sitting in the faculty room having a cup of coffee with one of his friends. Then Gary realized he was feeling too lazy to think about Randy . . . and that was the very character defect of which he was accusing Randy! Having reached that conclusion, Gary sighed and accepted that he was confronted with a choice: he could either tell the Zondervans what he saw as the truth—or tell them something less harsh.

2. Evaluate

Gary wanted to be a kind person; if he truly honored compassion and respect for others, how should he describe Randy's school behavior to his parents? Gary couldn't simply make up something positive to say about Randy; if he did that, he wouldn't be honest. If he wanted to be both truthful and kind, he would have to spend some time finding out what Randy's positive qualities were.

Special Education Teachers as Consultants

As more and more school districts find ways to include students with special needs in their regular education programs, special education teachers often act as co-teachers or consultant teachers with the regular education teachers. This situation demands that both teachers be able to:

- communicate openly.
- be clear about their education beliefs and expectations.
- define their separate roles.
- respect each other's skills and contributions.
- avoid being competitive or possessive.

Special educators who are consultant teachers work with students within the regular classroom.

Gary heaved another huge sigh and went to find Randy. He spent the rest of the period sitting quietly at the back of the social studies room, watching Randy take part in a class project. After only a few minutes, he noticed something that amazed him. He now knew what he could tell the Zondervans.

3. Decide

Even before Gary observed the class, his gut had been telling him he would be wrong to tell Randy's parents that their son was lazy. He knew if he were in Randy's position, he would hate to have someone say, "That Gary. He's just plain lazy." Gary asked himself how he would feel if tomorrow's front-page news was to read, "TEACHER GARY ROCK ACCUSES STUDENT OF LAZINESS." He had to admit, the headline made him uncomfortable.

Today's laws ensure that all school buildings are accessible to students with physical disabilities.

Living your life with respect and compassion for others is not a new idea. In fact, the Golden Rule has a history that stretches back thousands of years:

- Around 500 B.C. Confucius said, "What you do not want done to yourself, do not do to others."
- In 325 B.C. Aristotle said, "We should behave to others as we wish others to behave to us."
- The Mahabharata (written around 200 B.C.) said, "Do nothing to your neighbors that you would not have them do later to you."
- In A.D. 33 or thereabouts Jesus said, "Do to others as you would have them do to you."

4. Implement

When the next morning came, Gary was ready for his appointment with the Zondervans. He said hello and tried to make the couple feel comfortable. Then he glanced down at his notes from the day before when he had observed Randy interacting during social studies. "I've noticed something about Randy," Gary began. He saw Mrs. Zondervan suck in a breath as though she were bracing herself, while Mr. Zondervan looked bored. "Randy is always kind to others," Gary continued. "When others are impatient or make fun of someone, Gary doesn't join in. What's more, he takes time to say something nice to encourage others. I'm very impressed by the compassion he shows, especially considering that he has challenges of his own to handle."

A look of surprise spread across Mrs. Zondervan's face, and Mr. Zondervan no longer looked bored. "You're talking about Randy?" he barked, as though he suspected Gary might have confused his students' names.

Five Steps for Making an Ethical Decision

1. **Clarify.** Determine what must be decided and list your options.
2. **Evaluate.** See what character values are involved in your options. Consider the benefits and risks to everyone concerned.
3. **Decide.** Make sure your decision supports the Golden Rule. You might also want to consider how you would feel if your decision was publicized on the front page of tomorrow's newspaper!
4. **Implement.** Develop a plan to carry out your decision in such a way that benefits are maximized and risks are minimized.
5. **Monitor and modify.** Keep an eye on the consequences of your decisions as they unfold. Be willing to revise your plan—or scrap it altogether—if circumstances warrant.

Adapted from materials from the Josephson Institute of Ethics, 4640 Admiralty Way, Suite 1001, Marina del Rey, California 90292.

Gary nodded. "Yes. You have reason to be very proud of your son. Children his age are often very unkind to each other. You must have taught Randy well."

"I doubt I've taught him anything," Mr. Zondervan muttered. "All he wants to do is talk about dogs. The boy never wants to move, never wants to go anywhere, never wants to do anything. He just sits there like a big lump. I never saw a lazier kid."

But Mrs. Zondervan leaned toward Gary, her face pink with pleasure. "No one has ever told us we should be proud of Randy," she said softly. She smiled at her husband. "He *is* kind, Norm. I never thought of it before."

When a student with multiple handicaps has a physical disability, that may be what is most obvious. Special education teachers, however, must be able to see the whole child (not just the wheelchair).

5. Monitor and Modify

That afternoon when Gary went home from school, he found himself smiling whenever he thought of Randy. Randy still smelled bad, of course, and he still liked to talk about dogs, and he still was one of the most unmotivated students Gary had ever met. None of that had changed.

But Gary had discussed these problems with the Zondervans, and he now had a few new ideas for motivating Randy to focus more on his schoolwork. Randy's mother had suggested that her son might be pleased if he received dog stickers on homework he completed—and she thought he would do almost anything, include shower daily, for a glossy magazine filled with pictures of dogs. The Zondervans and Gary would work together on this new system of rewards.

Gary wondered if Mrs. Zondervan would have hit upon such a good idea if she hadn't been feeling so warmed by the realization that her son had an important positive quality. As the parent of a child with disabilities, she had years of experience hearing teachers complain about Randy. But today, for the first time, she had heard someone say something positive—and as a result, she too had looked at her son in a new way. And her new attitude had the power to influence both Randy and his father.

That didn't mean Randy's problems would be solved overnight. But Gary knew he and the Zondervans had taken a small step in the right direction. Gary would need to continue to encourage Mrs. Zondervan's positive involvement in her son's education; he would also need to monitor his own attitude toward Randy. The small step taken that morning would need to be followed up with other small steps, and that would take thought and effort on Gary's part.

That's what special education was all about, Gary realized—taking tiny steps of respect and compassion, one after another, until one day you turned around and were surprised to see just how far you had gone. His own actions had made that first small step possible. He was glad he had made the effort to be kind.

No act of kindness, no matter how small, is ever wasted.

—Aesop

Life is not so short but that there is always time enough for courtesy.

—Ralph Waldo Emerson

Many students with disabilities are mainstreamed into regular education classrooms. A resource teacher offers support to these students as they handle the frustrations they encounter.

4

JUSTICE AND FAIRNESS

When two character values compete—
like compassion and fairness, for instance—
you need to make your own moral decision.
There is no rule book to consult.

Sometimes it's hard to be fair. That's what Jenny Chen discovered early in her career as a special education teacher.

As a high school *resource room* teacher, Jenny's job was to meet with students with learning disabilities for one or two periods a day, three or four at a time. The rest of the school day, the students were in a regular high school program, but they came to Jenny for help dealing with their specific learning problems. Jenny worked with them on their math, reading, and writing. She also was an *advocate* for her students with the regular education teachers, and she made sure each student's Individualized Education Plan (IEP) was carried out.

Many of her students' IEPs called for them to receive testing modifications. This meant that because of their problems with reading or writing, they were allowed to take tests in the resource room. There they could have extra time to understand the tests, and Jenny read the test questions out loud to them; some of them dictated their answers to her. These test modifications ensured that their disabilities in reading comprehension or written expression would not lower their scores; the tests would measure their understanding of social

Students who attend a resource room may need to practice basic math skills. Each student's needs will be different.

studies or science or whatever, rather than their reading or writing abilities.

Some of the regular education teachers resented the fact that Jenny's students took their tests outside of the regular classroom. These teachers believed this gave the resource room students an unfair advantage. From the teachers' perspective, many of Jenny's students appeared to be simply lazy, uncooperative, or not very bright. When her students consistently performed so much better on the work they did in the resource room, one teacher even accused Jenny of supplying her students with the answers. "It's just not fair," he insisted.

Jenny worked hard to explain her students' disabilities to the regular education teachers. She knew her students did better in the resource room because they could get help there in overcoming their specific disabilities. She also knew that because she consistently praised their efforts and worked to make them feel good about themselves, they felt more relaxed and comfortable when they were with her—and their lack of tension also helped them to perform at their best. When she administered their tests to them, she worked hard at being completely fair.

> People who value justice and fairness:
>
> • treat all people the same (as much as possible).
> • are open-minded; they are willing to listen to the points of views of others and try to understand.
> • consider carefully before making decisions that affect others.
> • don't take advantage of others' mistakes.
> • don't take more than their fair share.
> • cooperate with others.
> • recognize the uniqueness and value of each individual.
>
> Adapted from material from the Character Counts Coalition, 4640 Admiralty Way, Suite 1001, Marina del Rey, California 90292.

But during Jenny's second year of teaching she ran into an ethical dilemma. One of her students was also the star football player. Although Jason could barely read or write, he shone on the football field, and Jenny understood how important athletics were to him. Out on the

The resource room gives children with disabilities an opportunity to work one-on-one with a special education teacher.

field, no one cared if he could read a history textbook, and his inability to write an English composition didn't matter at all.

But the school had a policy that all members of an athletic team had to maintain at least a passing average in all their classes, or they would be suspended from all sports activities. Every ten-week

Individualized Education Plan (IEP)

An IEP, mandated by federal law, is a written plan designed specifically for each special education student. The IEP spells out the specific education and related services that will best meet an individual child's needs, and the special education teacher plays an important role in creating this plan. The IEP defines reasonable expectations for achievement and specifies how success will be determined. It should include these points:

1. A statement of the child's current level of educational performance.
2. A statement of yearly goals or achievements expected for each area of identified weakness by the end of the school year.

The IEP is developed by a team that includes the child's regular education teacher, special education teacher, school psychologist, and usually the parents and even the child. The IEP must be updated each year.

marking period, Jason barely squeaked by with Ds in most of his classes.

Jason and his history teacher, Mr. Atkins, did not get along, and as a result history was Jason's worst subject. Mr. Atkins based a third of the final report card grade on classroom behavior, and Jason's attitude in class was less than ideal. To make matters worse, Jason often managed to lose his homework somewhere between the resource room and history class. Mr. Atkins had shared with Jenny that with a classroom grade and a homework average as low as Jason's, the only hope he had of passing history this quarter was if he managed to get at least a B on the ten-week exam. It looked as if Jason wouldn't be playing football the rest of season.

Learning Disabilities

Children with learning disabilities possess normal intelligence but may have

- difficulty learning to read (sometimes called dyslexia); 60-80% of all children diagnosed with a reading disability are boys.
- problems performing mathematics; about 6% of all children have this disability and most of that 6% also have a reading disability.
- an inability to express themselves in writing; students with this disability will also have a reading disability and most students with a reading disability will also have problems with writing.
- problems in all three areas—reading, mathematics, and writing; their disability in each area may not be severe, but when combined, their difficulties interfere with their academic performance.

Based on statistics and definitions from the American Psychiatric Association's *Diagnostic and Statistical Manual of Mental Disorders—Fourth Edition.*

But Jenny hated to see that happen. She knew a lot of things in Jason's life were going wrong. His mother and father were getting a divorce; his girlfriend had just broken up with him; and his best friend had moved to another city. Jenny didn't know how much more disappointment Jason could face.

So as Jenny read the history exam to Jason, her heart sank as she watched him write down wrong answer after wrong answer. "Jason," she said finally, "let me read question number three to you one more time."

Jason looked up at her face as she read the multiple-choice question again. One by one, she read the four possible answers slowly and carefully. He erased his answer, glanced up at her face again, and then

Excuses We Make for Unethical Behavior

- *If it's "necessary," then it's the right thing to do.* The ends do not justify the means.
- *If it's legal, it's okay.* The law sets only a minimal standard of behavior; being unkind, telling a lie to a friend, or taking more than your share of dessert are not crimes—but they are still unethical.
- *I was just doing it for you.* Sometimes we tell "white lies" or evade the truth to avoid hurting another's feelings—when in fact, although the truth may be uncomfortable, it will do the other person good to hear it.
- *I'm just fighting fire with fire; everybody does it.* The behavior of those around you does not excuse your lack of fairness or other unethical behaviors. There is no safety in numbers!
- *It doesn't hurt anyone.* We often underestimate the cost of failing to do the right thing.
- *It's okay so long as I don't gain personally.* Our actions may help some individuals; however, other individuals— including ourselves—are sure to suffer as a consequence of our unethical behavior.
- *I've got it coming; I deserve to take more than my share because I worked more than anyone else.* The Golden Rule applies here: would you want others to behave the same way?

Adapted from materials from the Josephson Institute of Ethics, 4640 Admiralty Way, Suite 1001, Marina del Rey, California 90292.

wrote down a new answer. This time he had chosen the correct answer, and she smiled.

He had missed question number four as well (and seven and nine and many, many more). Jenny started to read those questions over again as well, but then she hesitated for a long moment.

"Ms. Chen?" Jason asked.

"Give me a minute, Jason," Jenny said. "I need to think about something."

She wasn't giving Jason the answers, she told herself. She was simply letting him know which questions he needed to recheck. And he really needed to pass this test; how could it possibly benefit anyone if he failed? How could it hurt anyone if she helped him just a little more than usual? Without him on the team, their school would probably not make it to the championship. And even worse, without football in his life, Jason might turn to other more destructive outlets for his frustration and sadness.

Jenny knew she couldn't keep Jason waiting forever. Whatever she did now, she wanted to be fair to everyone concerned; she wanted to do the right thing.

What should Jenny have done?

The right thing may not be the easy thing. But it is still the right thing.

—D. Booker May

Some deaf children learn American Sign Language. These children will usually go to a special school where their teachers can instruct them using "sign."

5

RESPONSIBILITY

*A course of action that's good for one
individual may actually hurt someone else.
When that's the case, where do your
responsibilities lie?*

Everyone considers Jack Roosevelt to be a responsible person. His friends and family can always count on him to be there for them when they need him; he works hard at his job; and he always thinks through his decisions carefully. So everyone who knew him was surprised when they heard he was in trouble at work.

Jack worked as a special education teacher for hearing impaired children. These children attended regular classes in schools around the county; Jack's job was to travel from school to school, working with the regular education teachers to help them teach the hearing impaired students in their classrooms. He also met with the students, evaluated their progress, and helped write their IEPs. Jack enjoyed his job; he liked his students, and he got along well with the other teachers in the districts where he worked. He was grateful for the freedom to move around and set his own schedule. But he had become increasingly concerned about a student in one of the districts where he worked.

Six-year-old Aisha Temple had recently been diagnosed with a hearing problem. Until the diagnosis, her parents and teachers had assumed she had problems learning; her kindergarten teacher had

A student with a hearing impairment may learn better when she works one-on-one with a teacher who is seated close enough to her for her to hear him clearly.

even gone so far as to tell the Temples their daughter was mildly retarded. As it turned out, though, Aisha's intelligence was above normal; she simply could not hear what was going on in the world around her.

Aisha now wore a hearing aid that helped her a great deal, but she still had problems focusing on the teacher's voice. Jack had asked the teacher to be sure Aisha was seated at the front of the classroom, where she would have an unobstructed view of the teacher's face; watching people's lips when they spoke helped Aisha better understand what they were saying. At Aisha's last IEP meeting, the special education committee had also determined that Aisha would benefit from the teacher wearing a special microphone that would send her voice directly to a hearing aid in Aisha's ear.

The equipment was expensive, though, and Aisha's school was a small one without much money. More than half of the school year had come and gone, and the special equipment for Aisha had still not been purchased. When Jack complained to the school's administrators, he was assured they would purchase the equipment eventually, but each time they had a new excuse as to why they had not done so yet.

Meanwhile, Aisha was struggling more and more to keep up with the other children in her class. The room was poorly lit, so Aisha could not see the faces of those speaking around her, and to make matters worse, the classroom was next to the band room; the noise of musical

People who value responsibility:

- think before they act; they consider the possible consequences of their actions.
- accept responsibility for the consequences of their choices.
- don't blame others for their mistakes or take credit for others' achievements.
- don't make excuses.
- set a good example for others.
- pursue excellence in all they do.
- do the best with what they have.
- are dependable; others can rely on them.

Adapted from material from the Character Counts Coalition, 4640 Admiralty Way, Suite 1001, Marina del Rey, California 90292.

Computers and headphones offer a learning option to students with hearing impairments.

Due Process Rights

Sooner or later, parents and school districts may not agree on what is best for a child with special needs. In these cases, federal and state laws provide both the school and the parents with *due process rights*. After informal conferences or mediation, an impartial third party conducts a hearing to decide on the issues involved. Evidence is submitted and witnesses are questioned until a decision is reached—but this decision may then be appealed through the court system.

The education of children with disabilities is shaped by these court decisions. A variety of Supreme Court decisions address the issues involved with special education, such as discipline and the inclusion of students with special needs into "regular" classrooms.

The Price of Doing What's Right

Doing the right thing doesn't mean a person will always win in life. In fact, sometimes when people do the ethical thing, they may face consequences that are less than pleasant. (For instance, they may lose a job or a friendship they value.) But if people value what's right, then they understand their responsibility in life is not to win but to pursue the qualities found in a good character; those qualities will be the ground rules for their decision making, not just factors to consider. People who are unwilling to lose have to be willing to do whatever it takes to win. The truth is, losing is okay; in fact, it is better to lose than to lie, be unkind, or be unfair in order to win.

A good character has a price, and sometimes people must choose between what they want to *have* and what they want to *be*. Our culture often puts more value on *having* than on *being*—but once you choose to let go of winning and having, qualities like integrity, compassion, justice, and responsibility become worthwhile.

instruments could be clearly heard through the wall. In a large and noisy class of 30 other first-graders, Aisha was lost. She simply could not understand much of what was going on around her.

Jack felt deeply his responsibility to do all he could to ensure that Aisha learned and thrived. When his complaints to the teacher and administration brought no results, Jack thought through his options carefully, following the same steps Gary did in chapter 3. First, Jack *clarified* in his own mind the moral dilemma he faced; next he *evaluated* the situation, considering the consequences of various alternatives; finally he *decided* what to do and made a plan to *implement* his decision. He went to Mr. and Mrs. Temple and informed them of the situation. "Aisha is not receiving the educational program spelled out in her IEP," he finished.

Mrs. Temple looked troubled. "What can we do?"

A student with a hearing impairment may have difficulty fitting into his peers' social world.

Jack explained to them their legal rights as parents of a child with special needs. In the end, the Temples decided to file for an impartial hearing that would evaluate the school district's responsibility to Aisha. Jack supported them each step of the way through the legal process.

Jack's supervisors, however, were far from happy when they learned of Jack's role in the events. "How could you, Jack?" one supervisor asked him, her face creased with disapproval. "Why would you egg the Temples on like that? You must have known you were forcing the school district to take on the expense and risk of legal proceedings."

Jack began to explain that Aisha's IEP was clearly not being carried out by the district, but his supervisor interrupted him. "They're doing the best they can, Jack. Their budget was voted down again this year, and the money simply isn't there. What do you want them to do? Didn't you feel any sense of responsibility to support the district?"

Jack shook his head. "My responsibility is to Aisha." He got up and left the supervisor's office.

Following the five steps outlined in chapter two, Jack still needs to *modify and monitor* the decision he made. As he listens to other points of view and better understands the consequences of his actions, do you think he will still feel he took the responsible course of action?

I am only one, but still, I am one. I cannot do everything but I can do something. And, because I cannot do everything, I will not refuse to do what I can.

—Edward Everett Hale

Children with autism are socially withdrawn.

6

COURAGE

*If you follow the path of good character,
you must sort out for yourself the
consequences of your actions . . . you can't
simply do what others want you to do.*

S ometimes being a person of character takes courage. Liz McDonald
never thought of herself as particularly brave—but when it came to
protecting the well-being of one of her students, she knew she had no
option but to stand up for what she felt was right.

Liz teaches a class of six children in a private rehabilitation center.
Most of these children have varying degrees of autism, while one student has severe mental retardation. Two of her students, Samantha and
Richard, can busy themselves endlessly with puzzles; and almost all of
them love the old-fashioned record player. Spinning objects fascinate
them; they love to tap the table or repeat the same noises over and over.
Derek and Miguel are prone to banging their heads against the wall and
have to be protected from hurting themselves; Melissa has a distressing
tendency to bite others when she gets too excited, and Dougie hoots
like a monkey whenever life provides too much stimulation. His voice
will climb higher while his hoots come faster and faster as he works
himself into a frenzy. Liz has learned that hooting episodes can be
avoided if she keeps the environment calm and soothing; once Dougie
begins to hoot, however, nothing stops him except exhaustion.

Of the six children, Richard is the highest functioning. He has a milder form of autism often called Asperger's Syndrome. Although he is very intelligent, he seems locked behind a wall that prevents him from understanding or responding to the world around him. Some days he stares intently into Liz's face for entire hours at a time, making her uncomfortable with his fixed, intense gaze—but other days he seems unable to meet her eyes at all. He has memorized to the minute the times that trains pass by the building, and he draws elaborate, detailed pictures of the machinery inside a train engine. Some days Liz finds him in a corner of the room, repeating a series of leg jerks, finger twitches, and arm cycling. When she finally persuades him to tell her what he is doing, he tells her he is pretending to be the gear shaft inside a train engine or the axle between the wheels.

> **People who value courage:**
>
> - say what's right (even when no one agrees with them).
> - do the right thing (even when it's hard).
> - follow their conscience instead of the crowd.

A child with autism may be able to read and write—but she may be unable to express her knowledge to the world around her.

The emotions of a child with autism are frequently powerful and puzzling. Special education teachers who work with these students need the courage to stand up for children who are often unable to express themselves.

As the year progresses, Liz gradually coaxed Richard to allow her into his world, and he made definite progress in his ability to express himself appropriately to others. His academic achievements are truly amazing, for he memorizes entire passages of books and he has a grasp of science and mathematics that is far beyond his years.

But one day when he came to school, instead of taking his usual seat, he curled up in the corner in a small tight ball. When Liz finally managed to take his coat off him, she discovered three black bruises across his arms.

"What happened, Richard?" she asked.

"The broom hit me," he answered softly. His eyes filled with tears, and he hunched his shoulder as though he expected yet another blow to fall. When Liz laid her hand gently on his shoulder, he flinched away.

Later that day, Liz told another teacher what had happened. "I'm going to call the child abuse hotline and report what happened," she concluded.

The other teacher shook her head. "I wouldn't do that if I were you.

Richard's father is a lawyer, and his mother is a child psychologist. They're both leading members of the community. You could land yourself in hot water. Besides, it could have been an accident. Who knows, with Richard? Anyway, Richard's doing well in your class. If Social Services gets involved, they could end up moving him somewhere else. You know how Richard would hate to have his life upended like that. Routine is so important to him."

Liz nodded her head slowly. The other teacher was right: Richard needed stability in his life; he needed to know things would happen every day at a certain time and that he could depend on his physical environment staying the same. Even small changes in the classroom, like moving the globe from the table to the shelf, upset him. Liz decided to ask the center's supervisor for his advice.

"I wouldn't normally say this," the supervisor told her, "but this time, Liz, I'd rather you didn't report the incident to the Department of Social Services. I don't think it will do any good, and it may do real harm."

Back in the classroom, Liz tried to persuade Richard to tell her

Because children with autism are fascinated by repetitive, rhythmic motions, they may enjoy swinging.

Children with autism often live in a shadowy, isolated world. Special education teachers need courage and patience to teach these students how to get along in the world where we all live.

Children with autism

- are unable to relate in the ordinary way to people; even in a classroom, they are always alone.
- relate well with objects; they are often fascinated by objects that spin or can be manipulated back and forth.
- are obsessed with repeated patterns; they often will say and do the same things over and over.
- often have an astounding memory for names, complex patterns, and odd details.

Two to five children out of every 10,000 born will have autism.

more about the bruises, but he refused to even look at her. "I have to watch for the train," he told her impatiently and leaned toward the window. "I have to watch for the train," he repeated. "It comes at 1:09. The train will come at 1:09. It will take three minutes and 45 seconds to pass by the window. The next train will come at 2:36. I have to watch for the train." Liz sighed and turned her attention to Dougie and Samantha. As she worked with the other students, however, she wondered what she should do next.

Liz had met Richard's parents and had found them both to be high-power, intimidating people—but after school that day, Liz took her courage in her hands and called Richard's parents. "I need to talk with you," she told them and set up an appointment for the following afternoon.

> **Children with Asperger's Syndrome**
>
> • have little interest or ability for interacting with peers.
> • don't pick up on social cues.
> • behave in socially inappropriate ways.
> • have limited use of gestures, body language, and facial expressions.
> • often have inappropriate facial expressions; they may smile when everyone else is crying or have a strange, stiff gaze whenever others are laughing.

Liz dreaded the appointment. For the rest of the evening and throughout the day that followed, her stomach was knotted with nervousness. When Richard's parents walked into her room for the appointment, their aura of confidence threw her off balance. But she took a deep breath and began talking to them about Richard's bruises.

Mrs. Farr, Richard's mother, nodded and looked rueful. "He fell down the stairs. You know how clumsy he can be. That's all part of his syndrome, as I'm sure you know."

"Richard told me a broom hurt him."

Mr. Farr waved his hand impatiently. "I'm surprised he didn't say he was run over by a train." He grinned. "You know how obsessed he is with trains."

Liz was finding their charm and good humor almost more intimi-

Child Abuse in Canada (substantiated incidents)
(10 out of 1,000 children are abused.)

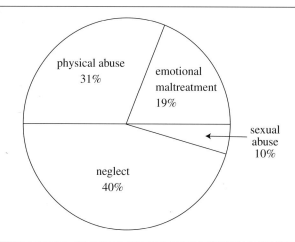

Source: Canadian Incidence Study of Reported Child Abuse and Neglect, 2000.

Child Abuse in the United States
(16 out of 1,000 children are abused.)

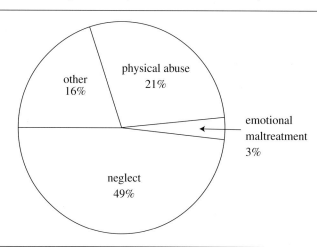

Source: Committee to Prevent Child Abuse, 1994.

dating than their air of self-confidence, but she drew another deep breath. "Richard has been unusually upset and not himself. I'd like to ask Social Services' help. A Child Protective worker might help us understand what's bothering Richard."

The smiles faded from the Farrs' faces. "Are you talking about a child abuse investigation?" Mrs. Farr asked, her eyebrows raised in disbelief.

Mr. Farr's gaze was cold. "Such an investigation could have serious professional consequences for us both, but particularly for my wife. Surely you wouldn't be so foolish as to start something like that when you have so little cause for suspicion."

Liz thought about the misery and fear she had seen in Richard's face; had she just imagined it? "Are there other adults in the household?" she asked slowly. "Perhaps a housekeeper or—"

Mr. Farr cut her off before she could finish. "No one in our home would hurt Richard. You need to drop this before it goes any further." The gaze he turned on Liz was nearly as fixed and intense as his son's. "Do you understand?"

That evening Liz continued to ponder the situation. Everyone, including Richard's own parents, was convinced that Social Services did not need to be involved. Liz was afraid to trust her own judgment when so many other professionals disagreed with her. She was worried her supervisor would be upset with her, and she was frightened she might set into motion a chain of events that would ultimately prove harmful to Richard.

But as she sorted carefully through the consequences of her various options, only one solution to her dilemma seemed possible. Mustering up her courage, she picked up the phone and called the child abuse hotline.

Do you think she made the right decision?

To see what is right and not to do it is cowardice.

—Confucius

Special education classrooms need to be bright cheerful places where students can have fun while they learn.

7

SELF-DISCIPLINE AND DILIGENCE

*Sometimes doing the right thing over and
over . . . and over again is more difficult than
facing a more dramatic challenge.*

Y ou can tell you're a new teacher," Maria Torres said to Sally May-
field as they sat in the faculty room. "No one else would spend so
much of their time working on learning activities for that class of yours.
Don't you ever feel like your efforts are wasted on that bunch?"

Sally looked up from her plan book, but she didn't answer. If she
had, she might have admitted that she often did feel all her hard work
was a waste of time.

Sally taught a class of eleven elementary children with mental retardation, while Maria taught the middle school class for children with
the same problem. Their rooms adjoined one another, and so they each
had the opportunity to observe the other's very different teaching style.

Maria's classroom was always neat, the desks in orderly straight
rows and the books in carefully aligned neat stacks. Each student sat
quietly at his or her desk, bent over a packet of worksheets that Maria
passed out each morning. They were a quiet, good-natured group of
kids, and although they were young teenagers, they seemed more than
content to spend their days coloring their work sheets with the bright
washable markers Maria supplied.

Meanwhile, Sally's class was chaotic and noisy. The children's

People who value self-discipline and diligence:

• work to control their emotions, words, actions, and impulses.
• give their best in all situations.
• keep going even when the going is rough.
• are determined and patient.
• try again even when they fail the first time.
• look for ways to do their work better.

Adapted from material from the Character Education Network (www.CharacterEd.Net).

desks were pushed in an untidy circle, and science projects, art materials, and the brightly colored blocks she used for counting and math skills spilled over the desks and tables.

Sally had been taught in college that children learn best from hands-on activities; that seat work and worksheets only keep students busy and teach them very little; and that children with mental retardation need plenty of opportunities for social interaction. But last week another teacher had complained about the amount of noise coming from Sally's room. And Sally was

Children with mental retardation need to be taught more slowly than regular education students. They may need the same fact repeated over and over before they can learn it.

Students with mental retardation often enjoy the chance to express themselves creatively through art.

beginning to feel discouraged. Most of her activities never turned out quite the way she had planned, and she wondered how much her students were really learning.

She envied Maria the peaceful calm that filled her room. Maybe worksheets and colored markers wouldn't be such a bad idea after all.

Most of a special education teacher's work occurs in the classroom, interacting one-on-one or in small groups with a child. However, special education teachers are also responsible for large amounts of paperwork, documenting each child's progress. This paperwork is a necessary part of ensuring that IDEA (the law protecting these children's right to an appropriate education) is enforced. But filling out the stacks of forms and documentation means every special education teacher has a chance to practice *self-discipline and diligence*!

Teachers who instruct children with mental retardation need to make physical movement a part of their program.

They'd certainly be a whole lot less work. After all, it wasn't like her students would ever win any awards for their academic achievement, no matter how hard she worked to teach them.

When the weekend came, Sally spent all day Saturday thinking about the dilemma that faced her: should she continue to work such long hours designing hands-on activities for her students—or should she model Maria's approach and begin passing out the work sheets?

As Sally clarified and then evaluated her problem, she was able to come to a decision, and by Monday she was ready to implement her plan. She had realized that some of the activities she was using in her classroom were less effective—and that meant it was time for her to try something new. But that didn't mean she was going to keep

> *I long to accomplish some great and noble task, but it is my chief duty to accomplish small tasks as if they were great and noble.*
> —Helen Keller

her students occupied with meaningless busywork.

It didn't matter that her students would never go to college or achieve life's highest awards. They *could* learn to be independent adults who got along well with others. But to do that, they would need to learn the basic skills of reading and writing; they would need to be able to tell time and handle money; and they would need to be able to read social cues and behave appropriately in a variety of situations.

Those were the skills Sally could teach her students, and she would need to be self-disciplined and diligent if she were going to achieve her goals. She would need to keep going and find new methods when she failed, and she would also need to make sure her students had fun learning each and every day.

It would be hard work. But eleven special people were counting on her.

The American Psychiatric Association's *Diagnostic and Statistical Manual of Mental Disorders* lists three criteria for a diagnosis of mental retardation:

1. significantly below-average intellectual functioning
2. significant problems in at least two of the following skills:
   - communication
   - self-care
   - home living
   - social/interpersonal skills
   - use of community resources
   - self-direction
   - academic skills
   - work
   - leisure
   - health
   - safety
3. onset before age 18.

Fall seven times. Stand up eight.

—Japanese proverb

Students with visual impairments have unique educational needs.

8

CITIZENSHIP

*You can't hope for a better world
if you don't do your part to improve it.*

George Ahmad kept plenty busy moving between the seven school buildings in his city school district where he monitored the education of 22 students with visual impairments. He spent time working with the classroom teachers; he advocated for his students and acted as a liaison for them with the other agencies that provided them services; he made sure their computers, tape recorders, and Braille typewriters were all in good working condition. By the end of the day, he was exhausted.

So he certainly didn't feel like hanging around in the evening to attend a school dance. All he wanted to do was go home and watch some television while he relaxed.

"We really need someone to chaperone the high school dances this year," the social committee chairperson had told him that morning. "We're asking for volunteers, some new blood to make sure the same people don't have to do everything around here. Can you help out, George?"

George wanted to say no. The dances weren't his problem. He doubted his students even attended the dances. He'd never really become friends with any of the other teachers, so spending time with them at a school dance didn't sound like much fun. With a quick excuse

Braille is a tactile language that offers some blind students another tool for learning.

and a promise to let the chairperson know later, he slipped away to meet with his next student.

Sue Gregory was one of his favorite students, a bright 16-year-old girl who could see only a faint glimmer of light and shadow. Until this year, she had attended a private school for the blind, and she was having trouble now adjusting to the regular high school.

"I'll always be different," she told George when he asked her how her week was going. "I'll never fit in. It's like I'm here, but I'm not really a part of anything. Nobody's really mean to me, but they don't include me in anything either. I just look in from the outside."

"Maybe you should volunteer around here somewhere," George told her. "You have plenty to offer this place, you know. That way you'd get to know more people—and they would see that you really do belong here. You'd show them you care enough about this place to do something to help out."

Sue frowned. "What could I do?"

"One of the buildings where I work is looking for high school tutors for elementary kids. You could do that." He glanced around the room, seeking inspiration. The sight of discarded papers in the wastebasket gave him an idea. "Or you could organize a recycling drive."

"Me?" Sue's voice was high with disbelief.

"Yes, you. You're concerned about conservation and the environment—and you have great organizational skills. Think about it." He smiled. "You'd be a good citizen."

"What do you mean? What does being a good citizen have to do with recycling or tutoring little kids?"

George thought for a moment, trying to organize his thoughts. "I think if we're good citizens," he said finally, "we all work together. We do what's best for our entire

People who value citizenship:

- play by the rules.
- obey the law.
- do their share.
- respect authority.
- stay informed about current events.
- vote.
- protect their neighbors and community.
- pay their taxes.
- give to others in their community who are in need.
- volunteer to help.
- protect the environment.
- conserve natural resources for the future.

Adapted from material from the Character Counts Coalition, 4640 Admiralty Way, Suite 1001, Marina del Rey, California 90292.

Teachers of the blind need to offer their students plenty of opportunities to explore the world with their fingers.

community. You know the way a living organism has many parts, each one of them necessary to the overall health of the organism? Well, that's the way human life is, too. We all need to work together, in lots of little ways, or we will all suffer in the end. We can't just concentrate on

According to the National Federation of the Blind, a large and influential organization of blind persons, "the real problem of blindness is not the loss of eyesight, but the misunderstanding and lack of information which exist" about this condition.

Special education teachers who instruct children with visual impairments have a chance to be an advocate for their students. In other words, they not only teach their students—they also teach the school and the community about all that the blind have to offer.

what's best for ourselves as individuals. As good citizens, we have to care enough to get involved. And in the end, we'll benefit as well."

After George said good-bye to Sue, his own words echoed in his head. When he saw the social committee chairperson coming toward him, he quickly thought through his options.

What do you think George decided?

It is in the shelter of each other that people live.

—*Irish proverb*

If Leonardo da Vinci, the creator of the Mona Lisa, *had grown up in today's world, he might have been considered to be a student with a learning disability.*

9

CAREER OPPORTUNITIES

*Life's opportunities come in various forms . . .
and you'll miss some of the best ones if you
focus only on money and prestige.*

Thomas Kean, governor of New Jersey before he became president of Drew University, has a learning disability. He almost gave up in school—but some special teachers made a difference in his life. He said,

> I overcame my particular problem because of really wonderful . . . teachers, who care very, very much. Gradually, with a tremendous amount of hard work and patience . . . , they convinced me that I could do it. They helped me to compensate for whatever my problems were. They found a way around some of my difficulties and enabled me to gain for myself some self-confidence and some belief that I could do it.

Without those teachers, Thomas Kean's life would have been very different.

Special education teachers have the opportunity to make an enormous difference in the lives of children with special needs. These teachers have tremendous power—a power that can be used either positively or negatively. (In his sixties, Hans Christian Andersen, the fa-

Alexander Graham Bell, the inventor of the telephone, did not do well in school. Today, historians suspect he may have had some sort of learning disability.

mous fairy-tale author who struggled with learning problems, still had nightmares about a thoughtless teacher who had made him feel awkward and stupid as a child.)

Special education is a growing field. Through 2010, the employment opportunities for special education teachers are expected to increase more than the average for all occupations. The number of students with special needs is growing, and at the same time increased

About 453,000 special education teachers were employed in 2000. Most of them—234,000—worked with preschool and elementary children. Another 96,000 taught middle school students, and 123,000 worked in secondary schools. Most special education teachers worked in public or private schools, but a few taught in special education or residential facilities, and some taught children who were homebound or hospitalized.

Areas of Employment for Special Education Teachers in 2000

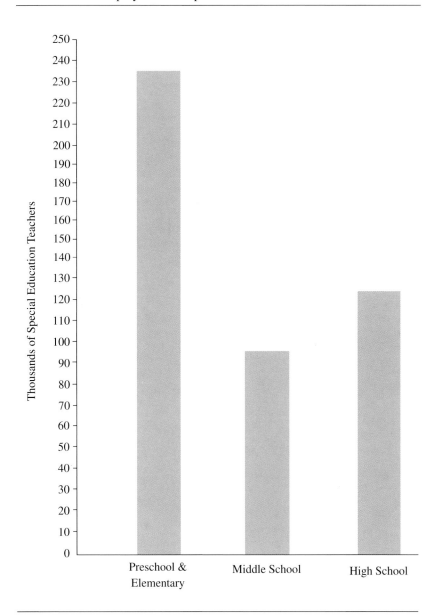

Based on U.S. Department of Labor figures.

Despite what may have been a learning disability, Woodrow Wilson grew up to become the 28th president of the United States.

legislation ensures that these students must be taught by professionals who can meet their unique educational needs.

Special education is not for every teacher; the field has additional stresses that cause some teachers to switch to general education or change careers altogether. As these teachers leave the field, they create still more job openings. Many school districts, particularly in inner cities and rural areas, have a shortage of qualified special education teachers.

This means the outlook is good for special educators entering the field in the next ten years or so. As the population increases in the southern and western areas of the United States, these regions are expected to have a particularly high demand for special education teachers. Job opportunities may be better in certain specialties, such as speech or language impairments and learning disabilities. Recent legislation encourages ***early intervention*** for infants, toddlers, and preschoolers with special needs, and this will create a need for early childhood special education teachers. As the population of both the

A special education teacher has the opportunity to make a difference in a child's life.

United States and Canada grows increasingly diverse, school districts will also need special educators who are bilingual or have multicultural experience.

Special education teachers earn between $26,000 and $67,000, depending on their region and years of experience. The average pay is about $40,000. Since most teachers have their summers free, many special educators also work in the summer (either in their school systems or in other jobs) to earn additional income.

With extra course work, special education teachers can advance to become supervisors and school administrators. Advanced degrees may also allow these men and women to become teachers in colleges that prepare others to be special education teachers. Some school systems also have programs where experienced teachers become **mentors** for those who are less experienced.

Torey Hayden is a special education teacher who went on to write best sellers like *One Child* and *Somebody Else's Children,* books that describe her experiences with children with emotional disorders. As an author, Torey no doubt makes more money than she did as a teacher—but her books clearly demonstrate the opportunities for joy and satisfaction that teaching offered her. Within her classrooms, Torey made good use of the powerful qualities of a good character, the same qualities we've discussed in this book: integrity and trustworthiness; respect and compassion; justice and fair-

> *If you are kind, people may accuse you of selfish motives;*
> *Be kind anyway.*
> *What you spend years building, someone might tear down overnight;*
> *Build anyway.*
> *If you find serenity and happiness, others might be jealous.*
> *Be happy anyway.*
> *The good you do today, people will often forget tomorrow;*
> *Do good anyway.*
> *Give the world the best you have, and it may never be enough;*
> *Give the world the best you have anyway.*
> *—Mother Teresa, educator of the poor*

ness; responsibility; courage; self-discipline and diligence; and citizenship. Because Torey lived these values and made them real, she changed the lives of her students forever.

None of her students have turned into tomorrow's Helen Keller. None of them even became the governor of New Jersey, like Thomas Kean. Most of them still struggle with very real handicapping conditions. Torey could not make her students more intelligent or fix the neurological damage that lay hidden in their brains. She had no magic wand to wave.

No special education teacher has one. But what all special education teachers do have are wonderful opportunities. . .

> **People who didn't do well in school who went on to success:**
>
> Hans Christian Andersen
> Harry Belafonte
> Alexander Graham Bell
> George Burns
> Cher
> Winston Churchill
> Leonardo da Vinci
> Walt Disney
> Thomas Edison
> Albert Einstein
> Henry Ford
> Danny Glover
> Whoopi Goldberg
> Jay Leno
> General George Patton
> Nelson Rockefeller
> Woodrow Wilson
> W. B. Yeats

- to demonstrate the integrity that will help children learn to trust others;
- to show the respect and compassion that will build children's self-esteem;
- to work with fairness, so these students will know they too are valuable members of the human community;
- to be responsible enough to teach students the skills they need to move toward independence;
- to have the courage to stand up for those who have often been rejected by others;
- to be diligent enough to keep going, one small step after another, so that one day students will look back and be amazed at how far they've come;

- to be good citizens, who use all the skills at their disposal to make their schools, communities, and world a better place for us all.

Education and training are important. Advancements and salary raises are achievements valued by any professional. But being a special education teacher means far more than any degree, title, or salary figure. The ability to make the world a better place can't be measured.

And it's character that makes all the difference!

Character is power.

—Booker T. Washington,
late 19th century American educator

FURTHER READING

Hallahan, Daniel P. and James M. Kauffman. *Exceptional Learners: Introduction to Special Education.* Boston: Allyn & Bacon, 1999.

Hayden, Torey L. *One Child.* New York: Avon, 1995.

———. *Somebody's Else's Children.* New York: Avon, 1981.

Jensen, Eric. *Different Brains, Different Learners.* New York: Brain Store, 2000.

Josephson, Michael S. and Wes Hanson, editors. *The Power of Character.* San Francisco: Jossey-Bass, 1998.

Kidder, Rushworth M. *How Good People Make Tough Choices.* New York: Simon & Schuster, 1995.

Yerman, Jim. *So You Want to Be a Special Education Teacher.* New York: Future Horizons, 2001.

FOR MORE INFORMATION

Canadian Ministry of Education, Special Education Programs
www.bced.gov.bc.ca/specialed

Center for the 4th and 5th Rs
www.cortland.edu/c4n5rs

Character Education Network
www.charactered.net

Josephson Institute of Ethics
www.josephsoninstitute.org

Office of Special Education Programs
U.S. Department of Education
330 C Street, SW, Room 3086
Washington, D.C. 20202
(202) 205-8824
www.ed.gov/about/offices/list/osers/osep/index.html?src=mr

Publisher's Note: The Web sites listed on this page were active at the time of
publication. The publisher is not responsible for Web sites that have
changed their address or discontinued operation since the date of
publication. The publisher will review and update the Web sites upon
each reprint.

GLOSSARY

Advocate Someone who stands up for and defends the rights of another.

Autistic Self-absorbed and withdrawn from the rest of the world to the point of being unable to interact with others; the condition begins at birth.

Behavior management A program where certain desired behaviors are reinforced with a system of rewards, while undesirable behavior is discouraged.

Certified Formally licensed to do a specific job by the state or other governing body.

Consultant teacher A special education teacher who works with regular education teachers, providing advice as to teaching techniques, curriculum development, and behavior management for mainstreamed special education students.

Early intervention Becoming involved in the educational program for a child with special needs when he or she is still a preschooler, in the hopes that more serious problems will be avoided.

Emotionally disturbed Educationally, this condition means that a child's emotional difficulties get in the way of his or her ability to function appropriately in the school setting.

Least restrictive environment The school setting where a student with special needs can succeed while experiencing something that is as close as possible to "regular" education.

Mainstreamed When students with special needs are educated within regular education classrooms, rather than segregated into separate classrooms of their own.

Mentally retarded Intellectual ability that is significantly below average (an IQ of less than 70), causing an individual to have difficulties in learning and social adjustment.

Mentor An informal tutor or coach; an individual who shares his or her knowledge with someone less experienced.

Resource room A classroom where students with special needs can meet with a special education teacher for a period or more during the school day to receive additional help with the regular education program.